How to Get a Business Loan

Insider Help from a Veteran Loan Officer

By H. Bradley Stucki

Kindle Edition

Be sure to check out other works by Brad Stucki at www.amazon.com/author/hbstucki. Free Downloads are often available. Also, click "Follow" to be notified of new releases.

Note to the Reader: This publication is designed to provide authoritative information with regard to the subject matter covered. It is sold with the understanding that the author is not engaged in rendering financial, accounting, legal or other professional advice. If expert professional assistance is required, the services of a competent professional person should be sought.

Introduction: Who this Book is For

This book is for entrepreneurs and business owners seeking financing for a business, project, or idea. It's specifically designed for those needing more than $50,000.

If you're looking for $50,000 or less, the process is straightforward: visit a bank, credit union, or finance company and apply for a personal loan based on your existing income and credit score. You'll complete an application, authorize a credit check, and if your income and scores meet their requirements, you'll get your loan. Simple.

For amounts above $50,000, the information in this book applies. However, with strong income and credit history, you might qualify for a "signature loan" of up to $100,000.

Consider these options before diving deeper into this book. If you need more than $50,000 and don't have sufficient income for a signature loan, the strategies in this book are essential.

Chapter 1: So, You Want a Business Loan?

I'm a loan officer with experience at both large regional and smaller community banks. Throughout my career, I've approved over $400 million in loans to businesses of all sizes—from startups to well-established companies. My lending experience ranges from $1,000 credit cards to $50 million for valued customers.

This book is written with first-time borrowers in mind, assuming no prior knowledge of the lending process. Even if you're an experienced businessperson, this approach ensures you won't miss critical details that could make the difference between securing financing and walking away empty-handed.

I've kept this book concise and straightforward—no fluff or filler to artificially extend its length. The information is simple, direct, and practical. I'll use a case study to illustrate key principles in detail. While the business used in the case study is fictitious, the scenario is entirely realistic, and the value of the example remains intact. I use other examples, however, which are entirely real. The names and other factors have been changed to protect privacy. By the time you finish this book, you'll be able to:

1. Evaluate your own business idea
2. Locate and secure appropriate funding to start or expand your business

Let's begin.

Imagine sitting across from me at my desk. You've decided you want a loan to start a business. Here's how that conversation might unfold...

"Hello, Mr. Jones. Thanks for coming to see me. What can I do for you today?"

"I'm here about a loan. I want to start my own business."

"That's great! I help people start businesses all the time. It's one of my favorite things to do (it really is, by the way). How much are you looking to borrow?"

There's a brief silence. "Uh, I'm not sure."

"That's okay," I reassure you. "Tell me about your business."

This you feel more confident about. "I want to start a landscaping business. I've been working for my uncle, and he just fired me. I'm tired of working for other people. I used to mow lawns when I was a kid and I figured I'd get some money for lawn mowers and trucks and go into business for myself."

I pause, considering my next words carefully. What would you say in my position? Does this sound like a good risk for a loan? Not at all—and you've barely spoken a few sentences.

"Tell you what," I say. "I have this application I want you to fill out. Just complete the blanks. It asks questions you'll need to consider and that I'll need answers to before we can proceed. Once you've filled it out, bring it back and we can talk more, okay?"

"Okay," you say. You take the application and leave my office... never to return. Instead of completing the application, you complain to friends that this "lousy" banker wouldn't give you a loan. You decide that bankers are all crooks who take your money but never help the "little guy."

Sound familiar? This happens frequently.

Now consider this next scenario:

"Hello, Mr. Brown. Thanks for coming to see me. How can I help you today?"

"Well, I'm thinking of starting a business. I worked for a company that went out of business. I don't want to go through that again, so I decided I want to work for myself."

"That's fine. Sorry about losing your job. What type of business do you want to start?"

"I've heard it's best to purchase a franchise, so I've been looking around and I've chosen a franchise business that I think will do well in our area."

You tell me about it. I listen.

"What do you think?" you ask.

"Well, it sounds good to me. Do you have an idea of how much you'll need to borrow?"

"I think about $50,000. That's how much it costs for the franchise."

"Do you need to purchase any inventory?" I ask. "Also, will you need some working capital while you're building sales? Do you have any savings to live on while you're waiting for the business to build up sales?"

You stare at me silently. "I think I'll need some money for inventory. I also will need something to live on while the business is building. I have some savings, but not more than about 2 months worth. You think that will work?"

"Tell you what," I say. "Here's an application to fill out. Look it over, complete the blanks, bring it back, and we can talk some more."

You take the application and leave. There's a slightly better chance you'll return in this scenario, but not much. You feel discouraged and increasingly so each day. You figure you should start looking for another job. Getting a loan is more challenging than you anticipated, and there are many factors you hadn't considered.

These scenarios aren't far-fetched—they happen to me constantly. I've grown cynical. I used to dive in and literally "teach" applicants what they needed to do to start a business and qualify for a loan. I was enthusiastic, eager to help the "little guy" build their business.

How many of these borrowers do you think I was able to help? ZERO.

Why? Because I was working harder at starting their businesses than they were willing to work themselves.

If you want a loan, understand this first: you must do the work, planning, and preparation. It's not the banker's job to do this for you. If that's your expectation, you won't get a loan. Your job is to convince the banker that you're a good risk through thorough preparation, knowledge, and sometimes, persistence.

Put yourself in the banker's position. Would you lend money to the two examples above based solely on the initial interview? Certainly not. Remember that bankers are responsible for the money they lend. If they make poor decisions, they'll soon be job hunting too.

Now consider this final example:

"Good morning, Mr. Black. It's good to meet you. How may I be of service?"

"I'm looking for a loan to purchase a building and start a manufacturing business for the home construction industry. I'll be using a new technology that will reduce wood usage in homes by 65%, create more structurally sound buildings, and improve energy efficiency. With the current push toward Green Industries, I believe I'll qualify for some USDA guaranteed funding. I estimate needing about $380,000 for the building and equipment."

I'm impressed. Mr. Black is well-dressed (not in a suit, but he doesn't need to be). He has a binder sitting on my desk.

"What's this?" I ask.

"It's my business plan," Mr. Black responds. "If you have time, I'd like to review it with you. Or I can leave it with you if you prefer, and make myself available for any questions."

A smile begins to form on my face. This is more like it.

"Have you ever started a business before?" I ask.

"Yes, I have. I've been a consultant in the energy industry and owned my own insulation company, so I understand construction, energy efficiency, and what it takes to run a business. I operated that company for 15 years before moving to this area to be closer to my ailing mother. I sold the business to a competitor and will use part of those proceeds for the down payment. I'll also reserve some as working capital during the startup period. I estimate it will take about 12 months to reach the break-even point."

My smile grows wider.

"I have some time now," I say. "Let's look at your plan..."

To make a long story short—though I've changed the names and some details for privacy—Mr. Black got his loan. I was happy to approve it because he was well-prepared and had done all the necessary work. He understood the business and presented a realistic plan that gave me confidence he would repay the loan.

That's why bankers lend money: so they can have it paid back... with interest. That's how they feed their families. If they don't make loans, they don't eat.

Chapter 2: The "Trick" of Getting the Loan

The trick of getting a loan is understanding the why, what, and how of preparing your loan request.

The Why

The "why" is simple: You need to convince the loan officer that you can start and run your business successfully enough to repay the loan—with interest.

In the first two examples from Chapter 1, I wasn't convinced any loan I made would be repaid. Neither applicant had done their homework, and neither had experience running a business.

The What

For the "what," there are two essential areas of preparation:

1. A Business Plan
2. Personal Financial Information

Your Business Plan Should Include:

- Description of the Business (what is the product or service)
- Detail of the funding request (purchase, working capital, living expenses)
- Historical Income and Balance Sheet statements for past three years (for an existing business)
- Projection of revenues and expenses for the next 12 months
- Marketing Plan (feasibility information and how you'll market your product or service)
- Competition Analysis
- Clear explanation of how the loan will be repaid

Your Personal Financial Information Should Include:

- Personal Financial Statement
- Copies of Tax Returns for the past 3 years
- Resume/Narrative of Business Experience
- Credit Report (usually ordered by the bank)

The How

The "how" is simply a matter of gathering the information—and it's usually not difficult. In many cases, you can find basic business plan templates online for free. Simply Google "Business Plan Template" and you'll discover a whole array of free templates to use.

This book provides a general outline for your business plan, highlighting areas that deserve particular attention from a lending standpoint. Remember: the larger your loan request, the more detailed your information will need to be. By searching online, you can preview different templates and select one that best suits your business. I just checked—it's easy. Follow the outlined steps, and you'll be guided through exactly what you need to do.

A good loan application will also ask the right questions. Take time to fill it out completely.

That's why, in the earlier examples, I gave applicants the loan application and asked them to complete it. I knew it would guide them through specific critical questions. This way, they would spend time thinking through their own business rather than expecting me to do it for them.

If you need additional help, approach your local community college or university business department. Many campuses offer programs that help new business owners create business plans for free. I know because I've referred many people to our local state college.

Your community may also have an economic development office that can provide assistance and information. I'll explain more details using a case study so you can see exactly what I mean.

This book gives you all the information needed to do it yourself. Follow these guidelines, and you should do just fine.

To help you fully understand each component, I'm going to use a case study that will show not only what you need to do but also provide an example of how it's done. The example will be straightforward. However, your first time applying, you shouldn't be requesting a $1,000,000 loan (unless you have significant preparation to justify that amount).

Let's say you have a business idea you want to launch. I'm using a startup as our case study because startups are the most challenging to fund. This is because there's no sales history and no proven customer base. Everything you prepare for a startup will be an educated guess.

When purchasing an existing business or financing the expansion of an established business, you have historical sales and expense figures to reasonably forecast future revenues and expenses. In this instance, the banker will want to see the past three years of historical income and balance sheet statements. If you don't have a full three years of data, include whatever you have.

Now for the case study.

Chapter 3: Case Study of a Loan Request

Let's examine a business we'll try to get funded: **Natalie's Real Estate School**. As we work through this case study, remember to use it as a model for developing your own business plan and financing package. At the end of this book, you'll find a checklist to ensure you've included everything necessary. The more you learn from this case study, the better prepared you'll be.

Note: This case study is not an actual business. For privacy purposes, I'm not using real numbers. This is purely an illustration showing you how to assemble your funding request.

Put yourself in the loan officer's position. You're meeting with Natalie, a top real estate broker in your area who's applying for a loan to start a real estate school. For the past three years, she's been among the top 15 brokers in your market. She wants to diversify her income into something more stable, although she's earned good money and is projected to continue doing so.

Natalie knows the real estate business inside and out. She believes she can help others learn the business and succeed. Her plan is to teach students what they need to pass their real estate license exams and equip them with skills to thrive in the competitive real estate sales world.

The following sections will walk through Natalie's business plan and loan request, providing you with a practical example of what you'll need to prepare for your own loan application. You can check off each component as we go along.

Description of the Business

The business purpose is to start a real estate licensing and skills school helping students pass the real estate licensing exam and become successful in the real estate industry. Students will also be able to use the school to receive continuing education credits for license renewals. Over time, the school will expand into mortgage license training and contractor's license training. The school will utilize the internet as a delivery platform for student convenience, competitive advantage, and future growth.

The business will be organized as a Limited Liability Company. After consulting with her accountant, Natalie determined this is the best business structure to manage liability and tax consequences.

At this point, I'll outline the various business structures under which you can operate your company. For a decision on which ownership strategy would be best for you, consult with your accountant or attorney.

Business Structure Options:

Sole Proprietorship: A business owned by an individual. It's the easiest to set up but provides no liability protection. Not usually recommended.

Limited Liability Company (LLC): The most popular structure. It creates a liability shield, allows income to pass through to the owners, and provides flexibility in management and financial reporting. LLCs are relatively easy and inexpensive to establish.

General Partnership: A formal partnership agreement structure that doesn't limit the liability of general partners. This structure used to be popular but has declined because the limited liability company structure offers partnership benefits with liability protection.

Limited Partnership: Requires at least one general partner, with the rest being limited partners. Limited partners have liability protection and can lose no more than what they've invested in the business. They cannot have direct management responsibility in the company. This structure has also declined in use because of the benefits of the Limited Liability Company.

Corporation: There are S Corporations, C Corporations, and regular Corporations. S Corporations are most commonly used for smaller businesses with relatively few stockholders. They have less financial reporting, and income flows directly to shareholders. It's similar to a limited liability company but has more reporting requirements. A C Corporation is for larger companies, has more reporting requirements, and income still flows to shareholders. A regular corporation is for larger entities such as IBM, Microsoft, Disney, etc. Shareholders have no management say (other than voting at annual meetings). Income is often retained in the corporation unless dividends are declared and paid.

This is only a brief explanation. This book aims to help you get a loan, not determine your business structure. I recommend talking with your accountant or attorney to decide what will work best for you. Personally, I have a sole proprietorship, am part of a limited liability company, have owned shares in several S Corporations (and even one C Corporation), and own stock in several large corporations. Each structure has its place.

Now, back to our case study.

How the Loan Proceeds Will Be Used

Loan Amount:	$ 97,000
Disbursement Budget:	
Computer Equipment	$ 5,000
Video Equipment	$ 8,500
Lease Deposit	$ 5,000
Tables, Chairs, Desks	$ 3,500
Advertising	$ 5,000
Student Materials Printing	$ 2,500
Business Licensing & Regist.	$ 5,000
Office Manager (6 months)	$ 15,000
Teacher Wages (6 months)	$ 7,200
Space Rental (6 months)	$ 30,000
Utilities (6 months)	$ 1,800
Tenant Improvements	$ 5,000
Contingency	$ 2,500
Loan Costs	$ 1,000

The disbursements align with what they should be. Natalie has considered all necessary items for starting her business. The next part of her plan shows projected income and expenses for the first year. This demonstrates that she has thought through how her business will grow over time and how cash will flow in and out—crucial understanding for business operations.

To project your income and expenses, you'll need to make assumptions about your revenue growth and expense levels. Natalie estimates she'll need to spend about $35,000 before she can even open her doors. These items include computer and video equipment, tenant improvements, lease deposit, tables, chairs, desks, business license and registration, advertising/website, and printing student materials for the first round of classes.

Revenue Projections

(Pay particular attention to this section. It will teach you the principles of projecting revenues and expenses—which are critical.)

Natalie already has 7 students wanting to take the 120 hours of education necessary to obtain their broker's license. She's offered them an introductory rate of $8 per credit hour to induce them to sign up before her school opens. She has arranged the teaching schedule so the course will be intensive, taking candidates only 2 weeks to complete—with full-time class attendance during those two weeks. This means holding classes 12 hours per day, 5 days each week. On Saturday, she'll operate only 8 hours. Sunday will be closed.

She anticipates this first broker's class and only a few others will sign up during the first month of operations, and plans accordingly.

Her regular rate will be $10 per credit hour. Natalie expects to sign up another 5 students each month for the self-paced sales agent course (90 hours of education). She estimates 2 students will take the intensive course each month. She also projects another 4 brokers per month will take the self-paced education hours, and 2 will sign up for the intensive course. All students are required to pay for the full course upfront.

The state requires licensees to take continuing education classes. Natalie estimates she'll attract 15 students per month taking approximately 6 hours of continuing education classes (which can be completed via video, and eventually online through her website).

Notice how Natalie thinks through each potential revenue source and drills down to what she can realistically achieve. She has carefully considered her market, how many customers she can serve, and knows (with some pre-sign ups) the size of her market and how many students she believes she can attract.

Simply guessing at sales levels doesn't help—it will only hurt you in the long run. Be able to justify your sales projections. If you don't, you're gambling with your future. Don't do that! Besides, if you haven't carefully justified your sales projections, you likely won't get a loan until you can.

Expense Projections

Natalie has hired three part-time instructors to handle specific topics:

1. A lawyer friend will teach all business law and contracts courses, receiving a $400 monthly salary.
2. A math teacher certified by the state's Division of Real Estate will teach math-related courses for $200 monthly.
3. Another top broker interested in teaching part-time wants to see up-and-coming real estate agents to potentially recruit for his brokerage. He'll be paid $400 monthly.

Natalie will also teach, paying herself $200 monthly. The rest of her compensation will come from the school's profits.

She knows she'll need a competent office manager to essentially run operations during normal business hours. This person will sign up students, field calls and questions, and manage the school's books. Natalie has someone in mind—one of her current assistants who wants to be involved. This person will start at $2,500 monthly.

Each class will be digitally recorded for website access. Future students will be able to access these online for continuing education, and new students for their coursework (although a certain number of education hours must be completed live). This expense was already included in the video equipment budget.

She's also accounted for rent, utilities, website, and advertising expenses, which will remain essentially the same each month. She plans for equipment repair and replacement with a set monthly amount.

Importantly, she remembers to include the loan payment to ensure she can cover that expense each month. For good measure, she includes a miscellaneous category for unforeseen expenses.

Note that the first month shown below is the startup month. The second through sixth months are essentially the same because she has carefully considered and justified each operating expense category. This is something you should pay particular attention to in your own planning. In most cases, you can estimate accurately through bids, calling utility companies, or consulting with experts.

When creating your own projections, Google "Business Projection Templates" and you'll find an array of free templates. Choose the one best suited for your business type. It will prompt you for expense categories and income projections. It's not difficult, but take the time and effort to do it right! Mistakes here can be costly!

Completing these projections also helps you analyze your business model. Will it generate enough income to be worth the effort? What if you changed certain elements—what would the impact be? Using projection templates allows you to adjust parameters and see the impact on your overall business.

Note: Because of differences in e-readers, the projections shown below may not align perfectly. Don't worry—there's enough narrative information to understand the principles involved. Downloading business projection templates from the internet will give you the greatest benefit as you begin using them.

First Six Months' Projections for Natalie's Real Estate School:

		Month 1	Mos. 2-6
Brokers	Accel.	$6,720	$2,400
	Regular	$2,400	$4,800
Sales Agt	Accel.		$1,800
	Regular	$2,700	$4,500
Continuing Ed			$2,500
Total Revenues		$11,820	$16,000
Expenses:			
Rent		$5,000	$5,000
Utilities		$300	$300
Teachers		$1,200	$1,200
Office Manager		$2,500	$2,500
Advertising		$450	$450
Equipment Repair		$150	$150
Student Materials		$225	$225
Miscellaneous		$150	$150
Loan Payment		$1,400	$1,400
Total Expenses		$11,375	$11,375
Net Income (loss)		$445	$4,625

The expenses appear consistent through each month. Natalie explains this is because she has established a budget for what she believes the expenses should be. She has also allowed for monthly equipment and classroom maintenance, so she won't be caught off-guard by unexpected major repairs. This approach seems reasonable if her expense projections are realistic.

You can see that if her calculations are correct, she'll be profitable from the first month. The projections also show that loan payments are built in and easily covered (except for the first month). She plans to repay the loan over 7 years at 6% interest.

Will this actually happen? It depends on how confident you are in her projections. While this looks promising, it's not a guaranteed success yet.

Natalie has no teaching experience. She also has no experience running this type of business. Generally, the higher the loan amount or the more complex the business, the more previous experience becomes necessary. If you're seeking a $1,000,000 loan to start a business in which you have little or no experience, approval will be difficult. In such cases, your business plan must show how you've brought in people (either as managers or partners) who have that experience.

For example, a young man applied for a $4,000,000 loan despite limited industry experience. To address my concern about his lack of experience, his **thorough business plan** included resumes and work histories of his partners and management team, all with years of relevant experience. We approved the loan, but we wouldn't have if he hadn't adequately addressed our concerns about experience.

Back to Natalie: What happens if she only attracts half the students she projects? How will existing competitors respond when they see her opening a school? What assurances do you have that the loan can be repaid if she doesn't meet her projections? This illustrates how important it is to justify your projections.

Natalie excels at real estate sales. She has numerous contacts in the real estate industry. She also seems highly organized and has prepared impressive projections.

Projections for Months 7-12

Natalie estimates that after the first six months, her school will be running smoothly. Also, because of her expert teachers and accelerated programs, along with some "real world" education she provides, she projects a 10% revenue increase in months 7-9 and another 10% increase in months 10-12.

She believes this will be her standard performance unless she expands beyond her local area through internet classes—an excellent growth opportunity with minimal additional costs.

Natalie sees this as something she'll develop after the first year but wanted her banker to know about these future plans. She also mentions that she can easily expand into teaching mortgage broker and contractor licensing, though these plans aren't fully developed yet. She has classroom capacity at no extra cost and can bring in teachers as she launches these programs. Her plan is to establish the real estate school first, then grow from there.

Here are the projections for months 7-9 and 10-12:

		Mos. 7-9	Mos. 10-12
Brokers	Accel.	$2,640	$2,904
	Regular	$5,280	$5,808
Sales Agt	Accel.	$1,980	$2,178
	Regular	$4,950	$5,445
Continuing Ed		$2,750	$3,025
Total Revenues		$17,600	$19,360
Expenses:			
Rent		$5,000	$5,000
Utilities		$300	$300
Teachers		$1,200	$1,200
Office Manager		$2,500	$2,500
Advertising		$450	$450
Equipment Repair		$150	$150
Student Materials		$225	$225
Miscellaneous		$150	$150
Loan Payment		$1,400	$1,400
Total Expenses		$11,375	$11,375
Net Income (loss)		$6,225	$7,985

The numbers paint a positive picture. She appears well-positioned to repay the loan based on these projections. How accurate are they? We don't know yet. They seem reasonable, but more investigation (and justification to convince the loan officer) is needed.

Marketing and Feasibility

The next section of the business plan covers Marketing and Feasibility. Here, Natalie must demonstrate how she'll advertise her business to achieve her revenue projections. She also needs to show that her projections are feasible and reasonable. This might sound challenging, but it's not.

Feasibility is a critical component of your business plan. As with projections, Google "Business Feasibility Templates" and review the many free templates available for your specific business type.

Below is a blog post I wrote on conducting a feasibility study. While somewhat generic, it teaches principles you can apply to your specific business.

How To Do a Feasibility Study (copied from a blog post)

So, you want to start a business? Great. Will it be successful? Don't know.

Why? Because you probably haven't done a feasibility study. If you don't conduct one, are you willing to invest thousands of dollars and hundreds of hours on a guess? You're not alone.

I've met with hundreds of people who had a great idea (they thought) and were ready to dive into business ownership. Most hadn't done any research to determine if their idea had potential.

Those who do feasibility studies typically get funded and usually succeed. Those who don't usually fail within 12 months. In fact, 95 percent of all business start-ups fail in the first year.

Increase your odds significantly. Conduct a feasibility study. It's not difficult. Here's a brief outline of how to approach it:

1. Define your product or service

What is it? What need does it fill? Who does it help? This identifies your customer base.

2. Determine the size of your potential market

How many people need your product or service? Is that group large enough to support your business? Why would they purchase your product?

3. Determine your cost structure

What are your customers willing to pay? How much does it cost to produce? Include all potential expenses you'll need to cover. Can you make a profit? Is it enough?

4. Determine your competition

Who are your closest competitors? Why would someone purchase from you instead of them? Remember, you'll only get a portion of the market, not all of it. Is that potential share large enough?

5. Determine how you'll market your product or service

What is the best way to let your customers know about your offering? How much will it cost to get this information to them? Too often people ignore this step. In reality, there is no "if you build it, they will come." Customers can't purchase if they don't know your product or service is available.

6. Test, test, test

Before you ramp up, do some test marketing. Find and interview at least 10 potential customers. Verify if your research has been accurate. After explaining your product or service in detail, ask them:

1. Would you be interested in this product or service?
2. How do you think this product or service helps you?
3. How much would you expect to pay? Do you think that's a reasonable price? Would you purchase at that price?

4. Do you know who else offers this, or something similar? What about this product is better than [competitor]?
5. How would you expect to learn about this product or service?

Analyze the data. After completing your feasibility study, you'll know if you have a potential business. Your decision will be based on research, not guesswork.

Now, back to our case study. Here's how Natalie has determined her school's feasibility:

Natalie's Feasibility Analysis

Natalie knows from the state's Division of Real Estate that approximately 2,500 actively licensed real estate professionals work in her market area. Each sales agent must complete 12 credit hours of continuing education to renew their license every two years. Brokers must complete 18 credit hours. That's a total of 30,000 continuing education credit hours per two-year period. Divide that in half and you get 15,000 hours per year, or 1,250 per month.

Natalie's projection assumes she will teach 250 credit hours per month in continuing education. This represents 20% of the market total. With two other real estate schools serving her market area, she believes it's reasonable to capture 20% of the continuing education market.

Is that reasonable? What do you think?

Marketing Strategy

Natalie plans to reach potential students through postcards and flyers distributed through area brokers. She can obtain a mailing list of all real estate licensees and use it for postcard distribution. She plans to send postcard mailings every 6 months, making people aware of her school when they need continuing education.

The postcards will offer existing agents 10% off their continuing education tuition if they refer a new student to the school. Natalie believes this is the best way to reach new students. In her experience, most prospective agents first talk with a real estate professional they know. They want to learn about the profession and what it takes to become an agent. Thus, existing agents significantly influence which schools new agents attend.

Natalie expects to get the most value from her advertising dollars by working with existing agents. This is a strength for her because she's active in industry associations and well-known in her local area.

Market Research

Further research with her state's Division of Real Estate reveals significant turnover in active licensees. About 250 per year drop out of active status and approximately 250 new agents get their licenses annually. Additionally, records indicate about 100 licensees become brokers each year.

Natalie's projections include 84 sales agent sign-ups. That's 37% of the existing market demand. She's also projecting 72 broker sign-ups, which represents 72% of the existing market.

What do you think? Is that reasonable?

Natalie believes it is. She personally knows many of the principal brokers (those who own real estate companies). She expects these connections will help her secure a lion's share of new broker applicants.

Online Strategy

Natalie plans to establish an internet presence. Her website will be optimized for local searches by people trying to obtain real estate licenses. She has hired a professional web developer. Once she has taught and filmed a complete course, she'll upload the videos with an interactive system allowing students to take courses online.

Natalie will also offer free online sales training to those who sign up for classes either at the school or online. These videos will teach new and experienced agents industry "best practices," ways to increase sales, and ideas to maximize business income. None of her competitors offer this. Natalie has taught these sales training courses to packed convention audiences.

Competition Analysis

Natalie has studied her competition thoroughly. There are two real estate schools in her market.

Brian's Real Estate School

This is the older, more established school, operating for 15 years. It's where Natalie received her initial education and where she completes much of her continuing education.

From her observations, Natalie estimates Brian's school has about 85% of the market. The instructors are good but aren't practicing real estate brokers. They're teachers who, while competent, can't relate the material to practical examples as effectively as Natalie's instructors will—who are seasoned, practicing professionals.

Furthermore, Brian's school occupies an aging building with outdated equipment. It's also located in a less desirable neighborhood.

Brian has kept his rates slightly lower (which Natalie is matching in her projections) and reduces costs by not upgrading his teaching space or equipment. Natalie expects to take about 30% of Brian's sales agent licensees and about 25% of his continuing education customers. She also believes she'll capture about 80% of the broker licensees. Most current professionals use Brian's school only because there hasn't been a better alternative, which explains Natalie's aggressive broker licensing projection.

Brian's school offers online classes for both new students and continuing education, but the website appears amateur and frequently has technical issues. Natalie has experienced the frustration of being halfway through a credit course when the site crashes, forcing her to start over. She will hire professionals to ensure her web presence is much more reliable.

The Local State College

The college offers real estate classes and special night classes that apply toward the education requirement for obtaining a real estate license. They also offer classes for broker licensing, but the schedule is scattered, often requiring six months to fulfill all requirements.

Courses are taught by local real estate agents or brokers as well as business faculty. The teaching quality is mediocre. It's a standard classroom environment, not specifically geared toward passing the licensing exam. The classes also count toward college credit, attracting students who plan to make real estate their career. The online courses utilize the college's web platform, which is stable.

The college is very price-competitive, about 30% lower than Brian's school and Natalie's planned rates. She knows the college has a built-in market with its students, but she still expects to draw about 25% of the college's business through her reputation and free online professional training. Natalie also recognizes that most college attendees wouldn't normally be her customers for various reasons, but the 25% market share seems achievable to her.

Loan Officer Perspective

So, as a loan officer, how are you feeling? Are you ready to approve the loan?

From an experienced loan officer's perspective, Natalie seems to have thought through her planning well. However, her projections for broker licensing market share seem quite aggressive—and that's her biggest revenue generator. There appears to be room in the projections for her to make up any difference in other areas, such as continuing education. Some additional strengths will need to offset the aggressive broker licensing projection.

There's one other point you may not have noticed. Natalie didn't—or maybe she did but wanted to ensure she requested enough funds to get through the initial startup phase.

Look at the projections and ask yourself: Does she really need $97,000? Think about that for a moment. The projections indicate she'll be generating enough revenue to cover expenses from the first month. If that's the case, then the amount she really needs is closer to $69,000. She would have the startup costs of $35,000, and instead of six months of expenses in reserve, could she manage with three?

Would a lower loan amount make you more comfortable as a loan officer? Think about it. Your ability to "think like a loan officer" will significantly help you obtain your own financing.

Now, with the above information, you've seen all the aspects of the business plan you need.

Next, we'll discuss the second portion of a loan request: personal financial information.

Chapter 4: Personal Financial Information

The next part of your loan request addresses your personal financial information. You might wonder why this is necessary. Think about our case study—we believe the loan is sound, but some areas appear slightly weak. Loan officers need certainty. After all, they're responsible for ensuring the money they lend gets repaid.

Remember, projections are only educated guesses. What happens if the business doesn't perform as well as expected?

One way to strengthen a loan request is to evaluate the borrower's financial standing independent of the business. Natalie has a good business idea, but she also has a successful career. Will her personal financial strength support her loan request?

Let's say she earns $200,000 annually from her real estate sales. Her plan is to continue selling real estate, though she expects her income will drop to around $125,000 due to time spent with her school. What if you discover she has no other debt—no home loan, no car payment? This means her income, though reduced, can still be used to repay the loan. Does that strengthen her loan request in your mind? It certainly does in mine.

The reverse is also true. Imagine Natalie has a $500,000 home loan and a $35,000 car loan, with her income expected to drop to $125,000. Does that help or hinder her loan request? To me, it significantly weakens it.

Now you might say, "But I'm not a loan officer." True, you're not. But you must think like one to first determine whether your idea is viable, and second, to prepare a loan request that **will be approved**.

You might be tempted to exaggerate your personal financial strength. Let me warn you: people try this all the time. Loan officers typically verify your information through multiple channels, so you'll likely be caught. And when caught, your loan request will be denied.

You must build trust with your loan officer. It's far better to be forthright and honest. When people are candid with me, I usually work harder to find solutions. When they conceal information, I look for what else they might be hiding. Your banker can be a powerful ally—don't jeopardize that relationship.

This might sound self-serving for bankers, but consider this: your banker does this every day. They know about loan structures and programs you don't. Let them work for you. The best thing you can do is provide complete, accurate information and then let them help structure your application. If they see you're willing to work hard to provide the information they need for decision-making, they'll work hard for you. Remember, they get paid to "make" loans. Help them do that, and they'll help you "get" a loan.

I'll step off my soapbox now.

Where was I? Oh yes, discussing personal financial information.

Personal Guarantees

Most likely, to secure a loan, you'll have to "personally guarantee" it. This means signing a document stating you will personally repay the loan—even if the business fails. This gives the bank the ability to ask you to use outside income or sell other assets to repay the loan.

This is serious. But remember, you're agreeing to repay money you've borrowed. You expect to make all the profits, so you should shoulder all the risk. If you don't personally guarantee the loan, you're asking the bank to take all the risk for your business venture. That simply won't happen. If you want the loan, you'll probably need to personally guarantee it. But if you're confident in your plans and efforts, it will be worthwhile.

There are exceptions, of course. Some loans are considered "non-recourse," meaning they don't require personal guarantees. I recently made such a loan. This typically happens when:

1. The business is well-established and financially strong enough that it doesn't need the guarantee to support the loan request, or
2. The collateral securing the loan is worth significantly more than the loan amount, so the lender doesn't feel a personal guarantee is necessary. We'll discuss collateral in more detail later.

The business projections showing how the loan will be repaid represent what bankers call the **Primary Source of Repayment**. Bankers also like to see a Plan B.

As a banker, I can tell you that actual results rarely match projections. Hopefully, they're better. Usually, they're slightly below but close enough. Sometimes, they're disastrously lower than expected. This is when a banker relies on Plan B, known as the **Secondary Source of Repayment**.

That secondary source of repayment is your outside income and assets that can be used to repay the loan. This is where your personal guarantee becomes important.

The information you'll need to provide includes a personal financial statement, copies of your tax returns, and a credit report. But first, let's talk about another critical factor to your being approved for a loan.

Personal Investment

Bankers like to see borrowers with "skin in the game." They want borrowers to invest some of their own cash or equity into the project. This can range from 5% to 50% depending on the project. This "equity" or borrower investment can take various forms:

- Cash (most ideal)
- Equity in assets
- Prepaid project expenses
- In rare cases, "sweat equity"

In our case study, Natalie has $10,000 cash she's prepared to invest in startup costs. That's a 10% equity injection. For this type of loan, that seems sufficient, provided everything else checks out.

Now let's talk about the personal information you'll be asked to provide.

Personal Financial Statement

This is simply a listing of all assets you own and all debts you're obligated to repay. Most banks have their own forms that will guide you through this process. As before, you can also Google "Personal Financial Statement Templates" for free templates you can use.

Here's an example of Natalie's personal financial statement:

	Assets	Liabilities
Checking Accts	$ 3,500	
Savings Accts	$ 8,000	
Retirement Accts	$ 150,000	
Stocks and Bonds	$ 35,000	
Jewelry	$ 15,000	
Car	$ 20,000	$ 20,000
Personal Residence	$ 625,000	$ 350,000
Totals	$ 856,500	$ 370,000
Net Worth		$ 486,500
Income:		
ABC Real Estate		$ 200,000
Debt Payments		$ 26,400
Estimated Taxes		$ 70,000
Estimated Living Expenses		$ 55,000
Cash Flow to Service Debt		$ 48,600

Note that Natalie has $11,500 in cash, so she can indeed invest $10,000 in the business. She also has a $350,000 home mortgage and a $20,000 car loan. Her total debt payments are $2,200 per month or $26,400 per year.

This looks promising. She appears to have sufficient resources to repay the loan even if the business completely fails. But then you recall her income will drop to $125,000 per year. If her business doesn't cover the payments, will she be able to repay the loan?

Consider this table:

Income/Cash Flow:	
ABC Real Estate	$ 125,000
Debt Payments	$ 26,400
Estimated Taxes	$ 35,000
Estimated Living Expenses	$ 55,000
Cash Flow to Service Debt	$ 8,600

This doesn't look as favorable. What will you do? You still think this would be a good loan, don't you? As a loan officer, you want to make loans. After all, the bank expects you to make a certain volume of loans, or you'll risk your position.

There's a way to strengthen this loan request: take collateral (also called security). We'll discuss this in detail in its own section.

Tax Returns

Next in the personal financial information package are tax returns.

Tax returns are requested to verify income. Bankers have learned through unfortunate experiences that people sometimes misrepresent their earnings.

Our entire economy is felt the effects of "stated income" loans— where income wasn't verified for home loans. Many people received loans for homes they could never hope to afford. They lacked sufficient income, and no one verified it. In other words, they lied on their applications. In some cases, mortgage loan officers encouraged or even facilitated this misrepresentation. Either way, verification is now a step that won't be skipped. Be prepared for it.

Typically, you'll be asked to provide the last three years of personal tax returns, both federal and state. If you're financing an existing business, you'll also need to provide the last three years of federal and state returns for that business. This verifies both your personal income and the business income stated on your financial statements.

If you're concerned that your reported income won't support your loan request, that's part of the process. If there are legitimate reasons why your income appears lower on your tax returns, document these reasons and include the explanation in your loan request package.

Reasons like, "I get paid in cash for many jobs," will raise eyebrows because it suggests illegal activity. It also tells your banker you're willing to misrepresent facts to the government, raising questions about whether you're being honest with them. It's best not to underreport your income on tax returns, as you may need to demonstrate that revenue when applying for a loan.

If you aggressively claim expenses and deductions to minimize tax liability, bankers understand this and evaluate accordingly. Just explain it, or have your accountant explain it. I receive these explanations frequently, and they usually work out fine. We deal in "cash flow," not taxable income. We understand the difference.

Remember, if you've prepared other aspects of your business plan properly, weaknesses in your personal financial condition can be mitigated through methods we'll discuss later.

Credit Report

There are three major credit reporting agencies. Their names aren't important. What matters is that your lender will likely pull a report from one or all three agencies. You'll authorize this in your signed application. The resulting report provides a "credit score" with two components: the FICO score and in some cases the BK score.

The FICO score rates how well you've paid creditors in the past. A score in the 700-800 range is good and will be viewed favorably for a loan. If your score is under 650, securing a loan may be difficult. You might need to explore alternative funding options, which we'll discuss later.

Your FICO score decreases due to late payments, excessive credit inquiries, high balances, total available debt, judgments, etc. It demonstrates how well you meet obligations and indicates how likely you are to honor future commitments.

Banks will sometimes use an indicator called the BK Score. The BK score rates your overall debt level. Lower scores are better. A score of 300 or below is quite good. A BK score of 600 or higher is problematic, potentially requiring alternative funding sources. Think of a BK score as roughly similar to a percentage (though technically it's not). It indicates the likelihood of default based on debt levels. A score of 300 suggests a debt proportion of about 30% with lower bankruptcy probability. A BK score of 700 suggests a debt proportion of approximately 70% with higher bankruptcy probability. This isn't precisely accurate but provides a general understanding.

In our case study, Natalie has a FICO score of 814 and a BK score of 240. What does this tell us?

It indicates Natalie has an excellent history of paying debts and carries a reasonably small proportion of debt. This is a positive sign for you as a banker.

With this information, are you ready to approve Natalie's loan? Do you still feel slightly hesitant? There's one more factor to consider: "security" for the loan, also called *collateral*. We'll address this in the next chapter.

Persevering Through the Process

You might be thinking, "Enough already! I'm exhausted by everything required for a simple loan."

Obtaining a business loan of any size isn't as straightforward as getting a credit card. With credit cards, you complete an application and the bank checks your credit. If you have good FICO and BK scores and the amount falls within what they consider your repayment ability, you'll receive the credit. But financing your business this way means paying a much higher interest rate. You're also unlikely to get the amount you need.

Control your frustration and press forward. Consider the benefits you've gained from preparing your loan request:

1. You now have a business plan and projections that will guide your business management.
2. You've thoroughly analyzed all aspects of your business, maximizing your chances for success.
3. You've tested your plans with a skeptic (your banker), and if approved, you have a better chance of succeeding than 90% of other startups.

Running your business will be far more challenging than preparing for your loan—you already know this. Once operational, you'll appreciate the time and effort invested in preparation. Your work will be amplified and rewarded because of this planning and preparation.

Moreover, a well-prepared package will secure the best interest rate and terms possible. This alone will save you thousands in interest expenses compared to alternative financing. That's money directly in your pocket.

Chapter 5: Security / Collateral / Risk Mitigation

When a banker requires collateral or security for a loan, the purpose is straightforward: risk mitigation. If you can't repay your loan through normal means, the banker will sell the collateral to recover the funds.

Collateral comes in many forms:

- Real estate
- Stocks and bonds
- Vehicles
- Jewelry
- Bank accounts (cash)
- Copyrights and trademarks
- Contracts
- Even cattle and crops

Essentially, anything with value that can be sold to repay the loan can serve as collateral.

Your loan request will almost certainly involve a discussion about collateral. Start-up companies are inherently risky, making risk mitigation critical for loan approval. You should begin thinking about what collateral you can offer with your loan request.

Let's return to our case study to see how this works in practice.

Natalie's Collateral Options

As Natalie's banker, you understand the risks of starting a new business. You wonder what would happen if Natalie only achieves half of her projected sign-ups. Would she still be able to repay the loan? It would be tight and certainly not guaranteed.

Natalie's excellent credit history provides some comfort, showing she has consistently paid her bills. This suggests she'll do what's necessary to repay the loan, but it's not a guarantee—it still depends on Natalie's integrity.

There's another critical concern we haven't addressed yet, one that's especially important for start-up businesses dependent on a key individual: death or disability. What would happen if Natalie became sick or injured and couldn't work at all?

That's a challenging scenario, isn't it?

One solution is to require that Natalie obtain life and disability insurance.

However, if we can secure additional collateral to support the loan request, we'll have greater confidence in Natalie's ability to repay.

Equipment and Furniture as Collateral

Natalie's school will purchase equipment and furniture with the loan funds. She can certainly offer these assets as security for the loan. These items are listed in the disbursement budget at their purchase price. However, both you and I know that used computer equipment and furniture cannot be resold at new prices if the business fails.

At best, these types of assets might be resold at 50% of their original value—more likely 20%. Still, it provides some security. The estimated resale value of an asset in case of business failure is called "Liquidation Value." The amount a banker will lend against a particular asset is called "Loan to Value" (LTV) and is expressed as a percentage.

In Natalie's case, the new value of the equipment and furniture is $17,000. At 50% of that value, you would be willing to lend $8,500 based on these assets. That's a 50% Loan to Value ratio for collateral.

Other Collateral Options

What other assets does Natalie have that could serve as collateral? There are the tenant improvements. Natalie will spend $5,000 preparing her school for occupancy. As a banker, you can't really sell these improvements—they become part of the building and generally can't be used as collateral. What else, then?

How about the equity Natalie has in her house? That can be used. The drawback is that her house already has a loan against it. If you had to sell Natalie's home to recover your loan, the $350,000 existing mortgage would need to be paid first. Is that a risk you're willing to take as a banker?

Let's analyze this:

Value of Asset	$ 625,000
Prior Loan(s)	$ 350,000
Proposed Loan	$ 97,000
Total Loan(s)	$ 447,000
Loan to Value	71.52%

What do you think now? If you had to sell the home, do you believe you could get at least 71% of its value to repay your loan?

As a banker using a home as collateral, I typically wouldn't exceed 75% LTV to maintain safety. Between 2007 and 2011, home values dropped approximately 30% nationally, with some areas experiencing even steeper declines. If you had loaned at 75% LTV, you would have been caught in a difficult position! That's why bankers are somewhat cautious now. During 2004-2006, many lenders were financing at 80%, 90%, and in some cases 100%

against homes. They suffered significant losses during the subsequent downturn.

Natalie believes her home is worth $625,000. But can you be certain about that value? You only have her word for it. Yes, she's a real estate professional who should know the market, but how can you be sure?

If you said, "Get an appraisal," you're absolutely right! An independent appraiser serves as a neutral party determining the asset's value.

You can have various items appraised:

- Equipment
- Vehicles
- Jewelry
- Stocks and bonds (these assets have market values you can easily check)

Be cautious with stocks and bonds, however, given the volatility of financial markets.

Probably the only thing a banker won't require an appraisal for is cash in an account or publicly traded stocks and bonds.

Using Cash as Collateral

"Why would I use cash as collateral?" you might ask. "If I had the cash, I'd just use it instead of getting a loan."

This involves a principle called "leverage." Here's a practical example:

Imagine you received an inheritance of $100,000. This finally gives you the opportunity to become a digital cartoon animator. You develop a business plan and determine you need $30,000 for equipment and overhead to start.

The problem is you don't want to use your entire inheritance for the business. What if it fails? You also want to quit your current job and work full-time on your new venture, which means you'll need living expenses.

The equipment is specialized enough that the banker won't lend against it. It has very little "liquidation value," and there's no secondary market where it can be easily sold. Your house has decreased in value (like many others), and you purchased it when prices were higher, leaving you with no equity to borrow against. Your cars already have loans, and you don't have other valuable assets except your wife's jewelry—which you don't dare ask her to use as collateral for your equipment loan.

Instead, your banker suggests setting aside $30,000 of your $100,000 in a restricted account to serve as collateral. Because the bank has essentially zero risk (they hold the full amount of your loan in a restricted account), they'll lend you the money at a substantially reduced interest rate (typically about 2.5% *above* the interest rate they're paying you on your interest-bearing deposit).

In essence, you've secured a $30,000 loan at a 2.5% interest rate. That's an excellent deal. The downside is that you have $30,000 of your inheritance at risk.

Common Collateral Types and Typical Loan-to-Value Ratios

Here's a brief list of assets that can serve as collateral and the approximate loan-to-value percentages banks typically offer:

- Cash/Deposits: 100%
- Stocks/Bonds: 50% to 75%
- Accounts Receivables: 50% to 70%
- Vehicles: 80% to 100%
- Homes/Commercial Buildings: 75%
- Improved Lots (commercial or residential): 65% to 75%
- Vacant Land: 50% to 65%

- Equipment: 50% to 100%
- Jewelry: 50% to 70%

Chapter 6: Loan Costs and Required Reporting

Now back to our case study:

Natalie agrees to use her home as collateral for the loan. You have the home appraised, and she was right! It appraised for $625,000. So now we can go ahead and make the loan, right?

As a loan officer... I think I would.

However, there are several other factors to consider. There was the cost of the appraisal. There's also the cost of title insurance to ensure the home has a clear title so a lien can be placed on it (meaning it's taken as security/collateral for the loan). And there's the cost of producing the loan documents for signature. All these costs must be covered.

If you look back at the Disbursement Budget for Natalie's school, she had allocated $1,000 for loan costs. That's right—the borrower usually pays these costs, typically from the loan proceeds.

In business, your goal is to cover all costs and make a profit. A bank operates the same way. They try to cover all direct costs associated with the loan at the time it's made. They also have overhead costs such as the branch building, utilities, support staff, etc. The interest you pay on the loan hopefully covers these expenses.

Common Loan Costs

Some typical costs you'll encounter include:

- **Origination fee**: Helps cover the overhead discussed above
- **Document fee**: For preparation of loan documents
- **Appraisal**: To determine collateral value
- **Title insurance**: To verify clear ownership
- **Recording fees**: For filing legal documents

- **Courier fees**: If FedEx or UPS is used
- **Government fees**: Such as SBA or USDA fees for government-backed loans

As a borrower, you should know that all these fees are negotiable. As a loan officer, I never waive these fees unless I'm working with a very valued customer I've worked with for years or who has a well-established track record.

Here's a general idea of what to expect for various fees:

- **Origination fee**: 1% to 3% of the loan amount
- **SBA or USDA fee**: 0.5% to 0.75% of the loan amount (See discussion of government-backed loans below). This is on top of the bank origination fee.
- **Title fees**: These vary depending on the collateral
- **Documentation fee**: Between $50 and $800 depending on documentation complexity
- **Courier**: $25 to $55
- **Recording**: $40 to $100 depending on documentation complexity
- **Appraisal fee**: $250 to $12,000 (for large projects and loans)

There may be additional fees. Make sure you ask about these early in the process, and your loan officer will provide an estimate for your planning.

Back to the Case Study

You tell Natalie the good news. The title report is ordered, the loan documents are drafted, and Natalie comes in, signs the paperwork, and starts her business. Everyone is happy!

Here's the answer to an earlier question I raised about the final loan amount needed. In this case, I recommended approval of the full loan amount requested. I wanted to ensure she has adequate funds to get started. You can structure the loan so she draws only the amounts needed during the first 12 months, and then when the business stabilizes, convert it to an amortizing term loan to be paid off over the next 7 years at 6% interest.

Ongoing Reporting Requirements

But it's still not done. The loan officer will require that Natalie provide periodic updates on how her business is performing relative to projections. This reporting requirement will be stipulated and agreed to in the loan documents. Typically, this means Natalie will provide quarterly, semi-annual, or yearly financial statements on her business performance.

Keep in mind the loan won't be repaid for 7 years. Banks are highly regulated—they're lending depositors' money. Regulators check to ensure banks are treating that money carefully. Part of those regulations (as well as good business practice) is maintaining close watch over loans. Not every loan works as planned. The banker wants to ensure they realize as soon as possible when a loan is starting to go bad.

As a borrower, you might be tempted to hide issues if you're not meeting projections. That's the worst thing you can do. As a banker, I have much more flexibility to restructure a loan and make accommodations *earlier in the process* than when things have really deteriorated. You'll only be doing yourself a favor by working closely with your banker. It's their reputation on the line too. They have a vested interest in helping you however they can.

Chapter 7: Different Loan Programs and Types

This chapter will discuss various loan programs and types. It's not an exhaustive list but is intended to give you general background and familiarity. The loan officer with whom you work should have more comprehensive knowledge of what's available at their institution.

Now might be a good time to talk about choosing whom you work with. Having the right loan officer is as important as having the right loan. People make a difference.

Some loan officers will work hard, be creative, and help you achieve your goals. Others will simply fill time, be unwilling to advocate for you, or fail to think creatively. This also applies to the institution. Some banks are more aggressive and have a higher tolerance for risk. Remember, though, there's a limit to what they can do because of regulations. The days of truly aggressive banks are gone—they've all failed.

Government-Backed Loans

The first category of loan programs is government-backed loans. These are primarily offered through:

- Small Business Administration (SBA)
- United States Department of Agriculture (USDA)

These loans are designed to help smaller businesses and enterprises in rural areas qualify for financing.

Both programs assist growing and start-up companies by guaranteeing a portion of the loan, encouraging banks to be more aggressive in lending to these businesses. Currently, the SBA covers loans up to $5,000,000. The USDA goes higher, even above $10,000,000.

The guarantees are strong enough that you can get up to 90% of your project cost financed if you have an existing business, or up to 85% if you're starting a new business. The rules of having collateral still apply, though with a strong enough business plan, you may be able to get an unsecured loan backed by an SBA 7(a) loan (though that's rare). Don't worry about knowing all the ins and outs of these programs. Choose a loan officer experienced in making these types of loans, and they'll guide you through the process.

SBA Loans

There are essentially two types of SBA Loans:

1. **504 Loan**: Primarily used for purchasing real estate or equipment.
2. **7(a) Loan**: Primarily used for working capital loans, though it can also be used to purchase real estate and equipment.

To get these loans, you must be approved by both the bank and the SBA. Your loan officer should help you with the paperwork, but if you've been diligent in preparing as indicated in this book, you should have all the necessary information. You'll need to complete an application and provide personal information, but nothing beyond what you'd need to do with the bank anyway.

There are additional costs with an SBA loan. You'll pay an extra 0.5% origination fee on the SBA loan amount. This essentially "buys" the guarantee. That's a small price if you get 85% or 90% of your costs lent. It can also make the difference between getting the loan or not.

For more information, see the SBA website at: http://www.sba.gov/category/navigation-structure/loans-grants/small-business-loans/sba-loan-programs.

USDA Loans

The USDA loan guarantee program is similar to SBA programs, with guarantees of 80% or 90% of the loan amount. You also pay for this guarantee in the form of yearly fees of 0.25%. Again, that's inexpensive if it enables you to get the loan.

The USDA also offers special programs for renewable energy, job creation, rural development, etc. Again, work with a loan officer experienced in these loans to find the best fit. There's also a requirement that you must be located in a rural area.

For USDA program information, see: http://www.usda.gov/wps/portal/usda/usdahome?navid=GRANTS_L OANS.

Within each of these two main government-backed programs, there are different "types" of loans, which I'll discuss next.

Types of Loans

Amortizing Term Loan

With this type of loan, you draw the full amount at the beginning and then pay it back over a number of years. The payments cover both principal and interest, and by the end of the term, the loan has been fully repaid. Your payments can be structured weekly, monthly, quarterly, or annually, depending on your business cash flow cycle. This type of loan is ideal for purchasing real estate or equipment. It typically has a term of 5 years or more.

Term Loan

This type of loan is generally for 5 years or less—usually within 3 years. The loan can be drawn all at the beginning or over a short period. It's also known as a bridge loan. The payment structure varies. They can be interest-only payments or amortized over a longer period than the loan term—such as amortized over 15 years, but with the full loan due in 5 years (with a balloon payment). Payments are generally monthly but can be quarterly, semi-annual, or annual. In other words, it's negotiable.

Single Pay Loan

With this loan, you draw the full amount (to make a purchase or payment) and then repay the full amount—with interest—at loan maturity. This is often used for purchasing larger assets that are then used in a process or as part of an investment, and then sold for a profit. This helps align the repayment timing with the sale of the asset or investment. This type of loan is rarely used even with seasoned borrowers. I've never arranged this type of loan for a start-up business.

Revolving Line of Credit

This type of loan is very flexible. It's most often used to help businesses finance through a business cycle. A business draws funds to purchase inventory. Then when the inventory is sold and cash collected, the loan is paid back. The loan can be drawn up and paid down several times during the term. That's why it's called "revolving." The term is usually for a 12-month period, then renewed for another 12 months as long as the loan has been handled properly.

Standby Letter of Credit

This is a letter (loan) that the bank provides stating they are willing to make a payment to a designated party if something does (or does not) happen. It's often used to secure the purchase of assets or inventory in a foreign country, or as a surety bond. No funds are expended unless the triggering event occurs. Then the borrower becomes obligated to repay the loan under the stated terms and conditions.

HECL (Home Equity Credit Line)

I've put this last because this loan isn't based on business collateral. It's fairly easy to obtain if you have equity in your home and is very cost-effective. With this loan, they simply look at your ability to repay based on your current income levels. It's like qualifying for a home loan. It won't consider your projected business income, nor will they ask for a business plan—so be careful. You'll still want to ensure that if you take on the debt, you'll have means to repay (so you'll probably want to determine your business feasibility anyway). This loan works like a revolving line of credit but uses your home equity as collateral. Because it's based on a home loan, interest rates are usually lower (though not always). These loans can be the primary loan against your home, or what's termed a "2nd lien" or "2nd mortgage."

Something Different

There are many other types of loans and combinations of the above. Some banks (and bankers) are creative in their loan structuring. Others are not. Your best bet is to shop around for the right bank and banker for your situation. Find a loan officer who is familiar and experienced with many different types of loans so you can find the one that best fits your circumstances.

You don't want to purchase a building with a revolving line of credit. Nor do you want to purchase short-term inventory with a long amortizing term loan. Everything has to align for your business to succeed. If you have the wrong type of loan, you can be just as doomed as having no loan at all.

Again, work with a loan officer you trust. They structure loans for a living. Make sure they understand your business almost as well as you do, and they'll help you get the right loan.

Chapter 8: A Note About Interest Rates

Interest is the rent you pay on borrowed money. Remember, the interest rate you're charged is negotiable. However, if you're just starting out with your first loan, you don't have a strong bargaining position. The best way to secure the lowest possible interest rate is to shop around.

With your complete loan package in hand, you can approach several different banks, ask them to review it, and if they all want to give you a loan, request that they bid on the interest rate and fees they'll charge. Let them know you're shopping around—not in an arrogant way, just matter-of-factly. If they want your business (and most loan officers are competitive about securing loans they want), they'll give you a competitive bid. From there, you can choose which option offers the best combination of rate, terms, and service.

I know several examples where this approach saved borrowers nearly 2% on their interest rate, not to mention discounts on origination fees.

This single technique can save you thousands of dollars annually—money that directly impacts your bottom line. For example, on a $100,000 loan, saving 2% on your interest rate means $2,000 in savings during the first year alone. Over the life of a 15-year loan, the savings will exceed $15,000. It's definitely worth the time to shop around.

Chapter 9: The Checklist

Below is a checklist of what you'll need for a complete loan request package. Each bank will have slightly different requirements, but this list will help you prepare 90% or more of what you'll need. Requirements may also vary by loan type.

I've indicated when you generally need to have each piece of information ready.

Once you've identified which bank and loan structure seems best for your situation, gather the remaining items quickly. Taking too long to compile all the required information makes your loan request appear stale in the loan officer's mind. They might question your commitment to your idea, which could lead to hesitation in giving approval.

Loan Application Checklist

Basic Information

- **Official name** (or anticipated name) of the borrowing entity and its structure (LLC, S-Corp, Individual, etc.)
  - *Not required during initial visits. Prepare when needed.*
- **Entity documents** of the borrowing entity, such as articles of organization and operating agreement (for LLCs), or articles of incorporation and bylaws (for corporations)
  - *These should be file-stamped copies to verify they were recorded in the state where the entity was formed*
  - *Not required during initial visits. Prepare when needed.*
- **Names of primary owners** of the borrowing entity (all those with 20% or higher interest)
  - *Not required during initial visits, but good to have if possible.*

Business Documentation

- **Business Plan**: including business description, funding request details, 12-month revenue and expense projections, marketing & feasibility plan, competition analysis, and loan repayment details (essentially what most of this book has covered)
  - *Essential to have mostly completed during initial visits.*
- **Financial Statements** of the borrowing entity (balance sheet and income statement) for the past 3 years if available
  - *Good to have during initial visits.*
- **Financial Projections** of the business (projected income and balance sheet for at least a projected 12 month period. Ideally, you'd want 24 months.
  - *Good to have ready during initial visits or shortly thereafter.*
- **Debt Schedule** of the borrowing entity (including contingent debt) showing loan amounts, maturity dates, interest rates, and payment amounts
  - *Good to have ready for when requested.*
- **Tax Returns** of the borrowing entity for past 3 years with all schedules (if available)
  - *Good to have ready for when requested.*

Personal Documentation

- **Personal Financial Statement** of all guarantors (owners of 20% or more of the borrowing entity)
  - *Good to have during initial visits.*
- **Tax Returns** of the guarantors for the past 3 years with all schedules and K1's
  - *Good to have ready for when requested.*
- **Debt Schedules** of all guarantors (including contingent debt) showing loan amounts, maturity dates, interest rates, and payment amounts
  - *Good to have ready for when requested.*

Collateral Information

- **Description of the collateral** (Equipment or legal description of property)
    - *Good to have a listing of equipment types and prices or property types and prices during initial visits.*

For Real Estate Loans

If your business loan request involves purchasing a building, the following information applies:

- **Occupancy status**: Will the property be owner-occupied or have additional tenants?
    - *Good to have ready during initial visits.*
- **Lease documentation**: Copies of all leases or letters of intent (including leases to the borrowing entity)
    - *Good to have ready for when requested.*
- **Appraisal**: An appraisal of the collateral will be ordered by the bank. **Do not order it yourself!** It cannot be used because of federal regulations.

For Construction Loans

If your loan involves construction, you'll likely need to gather:

- **Cost breakdown** of the improvements
    - *Good to have at least a rough estimate during initial visits.*
- **Zoning verification** for the proposed construction
    - *Good to have during initial visits—or an explanation of how likely the approvals are to be received.*
- **Construction contract**
    - *Have at least a rough estimate during initial visits. The actual contract will be required toward the end when everything is near finalization.*
- **Supporting documentation**: Copies of title reports, soils reports, environmental reports
    - *Usually gathered during the process and not needed at initial visits unless there's a known issue.*
- **Construction plans and building permits**

o   *Usually gathered toward the end of the process.*

I know this list seems daunting, but the bank has a very good reason for requesting each item. If you have questions, don't hesitate to ask. Rather than fighting the process, simply roll up your sleeves and gather the materials. Your life will be much easier with a complete package. If you cooperate with your loan officer, they will work very hard for you. And then you'll have your money!

Chapter 10: Congratulations! Or Not

If you've gone through all the steps with your own business, prepared your package, presented it, worked through issues with your loan officer, and secured a loan—congratulations! If you haven't, don't give up.

You may have encountered several roadblocks. Let's identify them and consider solutions.

Potential Roadblocks and Solutions

Business Feasibility Issues

Your business may not be feasible. Perhaps your projections don't show enough revenue to cover expenses and repay the loan with a comfortable margin. If so, consider yourself fortunate that you didn't invest money in a venture that wasn't viable. You can always develop a different idea or refine your existing concept to make it stronger.

This is how most successful businesses evolve. It's rare that your first concept is the one you eventually implement. Going through this process identifies weaknesses and often reveals opportunities. Try again.

Insufficient Collateral

If you lack sufficient collateral, consider partnering with others who have assets they can pledge to the business.

I know several businesses with excellent start-up plans that couldn't get financing due to lack of collateral. They found partners to provide that security. In these cases, the collateral partner received a preferred return from the business until the loan was paid off, and then was "bought out" of the business at a pre-determined amount as compensation for the use of their collateral.

Poor Credit History

If your credit isn't strong enough, find someone with good credit who's willing to co-sign the loan with you.

Lack of Experience

If you don't have sufficient experience, find someone who does and either hire them or bring them on as a partner. Remember the example I gave earlier of the $4,000,000 loan given to an inexperienced young man. He overcame his inexperience by bringing in partners and employees with the necessary expertise. You can do the same.

A Word About Partnerships

Be careful when bringing in partners to compensate for something you lack. I've seen more partnerships fail than succeed. Whatever agreement you make should be in writing, with each partner committed to fulfilling their obligations.

That said, I've participated in several successful partnerships. They've allowed me to leverage my financial strength and resources to accomplish things I couldn't have done alone.

Still at an impasse? Convinced your idea is exceptional and unwilling to abandon it? Consider the alternative financing sources in the next chapter.

Chapter 11: Alternative Sources of Financing

Let's say you've completed all the steps above but still struck out. Yet you believe so strongly in your business idea that you can't set it aside. If that's the case, I applaud your persistence and conviction.

Here are several ways to raise funds outside traditional banking channels. This isn't a comprehensive list—just the most commonly used methods. There are as many alternative financing sources as the imagination can create.

As you explore these alternatives, remember you're assuming greater risk. These lenders may not require all the information a bank would, but this is typically offset by higher interest rates and stricter penalties for non-payment.

Important Cautions

Remember that you won't have the same regulatory protections as with a bank. You may encounter unscrupulous individuals, especially if you appear desperate for funding. They can spot desperation from a mile away.

Another critical warning: Avoid paying money upfront except for reasonable appraisal fees and possibly a small deposit on the origination fee. Try to limit your initial payment to just the appraisal fee, paying nothing else until you secure the loan. There are dishonest operators who promise much but deliver nothing—especially after collecting thousands in upfront fees. This happens frequently.

Alternative Financing Options

Seller Financing

Also called "owner financing," this is where the seller of the business, building, or asset you're purchasing agrees to accept payments over time. Generally, you make a down payment (your equity or "skin in the game") followed by scheduled payments. If you default, the seller has the right to repossess the asset (just like a bank would).

This financing typically occurs when a business or property seller recognizes that buyers may not qualify for traditional bank financing. To facilitate the sale, the seller offers to finance it themselves. This approach works well for purchasing a business that may lack sufficient collateral to secure a bank loan.

Payables Financing/Vendor Financing

This involves having suppliers carry the cost of inventory or materials until you pay them back. When you receive "net 30" terms on purchases, the seller is giving you 30 days to pay. If you can sell the merchandise faster than 30 days, you've made a profit using the supplier's money. If you can't pay when due, your credit standing will suffer significantly.

This can work on a larger scale too. I've heard of manufacturers delaying payment on equipment costing hundreds of thousands of dollars for up to a year while the customer puts the equipment into service and generates revenue. Usually, a deposit is required, but paying a deposit is far better than paying the full amount upfront.

Private Financing

This involves a private investor lending money based on mutually agreed terms and conditions. This ranges from a parent lending money to their child at favorable rates to a loan shark charging exorbitant rates to desperate borrowers.

This type of financing is sometimes called "hard money" financing because the terms can be extremely stringent or "hard." In some cases, the lender may actually hope you'll default because they stand to profit more from acquiring the collateral. Exercise extreme caution with these arrangements.

However, these loans serve a purpose. If you have a valuable asset, such as a large tract of vacant land sitting idle, you can use it as collateral. Hard money lenders appreciate these deals. They'll charge higher interest rates and more upfront fees, but you'll get the money based solely on the collateral's value. No business plan required.

Just remember—if you default, you'll lose the property. Make sure you can repay the loan.

Equity Financing

This involves allowing partners to buy into your business. They invest a certain amount for a percentage of ownership. The advantage is you don't face the pressure of loan repayment on strict terms. The disadvantage is sharing profits and potentially management control. However, to secure funding, some compromise may be necessary.

Final Thoughts

There are countless ways to find alternative financing—you just need imagination. The examples above represent the main categories, which you can mix and match to suit your needs.

Be careful out there. Make sure you consult competent professionals for any legal or accounting matters. The relatively small cost of these services can save you a fortune down the road.

Chapter 12: Case Studies

The following six case studies showcase different types of loans. These examples not only illustrate what's possible but also demonstrate what borrowers did to convince banks to say "Yes!"— or why they received a "No."

These cases also highlight the importance of finding the right lender. If the first bank declines your request, try others. But be prepared: develop a compelling repayment plan and show why YOU are the right person to make that plan succeed. Be willing to provide adequate security for the loan in case things don't go according to plan. Remember, YOU are taking the risk, not the bank. Don't expect them to shoulder all the risk for your venture.

Case Study #1: Business Start-Up (Medical Device)

Two school counselors and therapists with a limited private practice helped develop a non-invasive, non-drug medical device that helped children with severe ADHD focus better in the classroom and at home.

The product was ready for market, but they had exhausted their capital during development beyond the prototype phase. Now they needed funds to manufacture and market the product. They had secured a patent, collected test cases and testimonials, and lined up a manufacturer. They had identified their market: school counselors and therapists nationwide, similar to themselves. The therapists wouldn't purchase the product directly but would recommend it to their patients.

They needed funding to scale up marketing and build product inventory. Since the product was manufactured overseas—a months-long process—they needed sufficient inventory to sell while awaiting new shipments. They planned to reorder as product sold and shipped to end buyers.

As a banker, everything looked promising except one crucial element: security for the $250,000 loan. They offered the devices themselves as collateral, which seems logical, right? I would have the very devices the loan would produce as security. Simple?

Wrong.

Here's why I couldn't accept the devices as collateral:

First, if the devices failed to sell as projected and I had to take them as loan repayment, I would lose substantially. Why? Because if the experts in this product and market couldn't sell it successfully, how could I—a banker with no expertise in their field—hope to do better?

Second, they wanted the bank to fund 100% of production costs. Banks rarely fund 100% of anything. Why? Because if the bank must repossess and sell an asset to recover its money, they need a margin to ensure they can sell the asset for enough to repay the loan.

The Solution

Instead of using the devices as collateral, I suggested they each obtain home equity lines of credit. Both owned homes with available equity and had income outside of this venture to service the debt.

They followed this advice and secured combined revolving credit lines totaling $100,000. Though less than their original request, it was enough to launch the business. The amount was also small enough that, if the venture failed, they could repay the loans with income from their existing work. They would grow more slowly but on firmer financial footing.

As devices sold, they would pay down their credit lines, creating available funding for the next manufacturing order. Over time, they would set aside profits to fund larger orders until the business became self-funding.

Why They Got the Loan

- They had experience in their field
- They had identified and quantified their target market
- They had a competitive advantage (a patented device)
- We identified adequate collateral
- The loan amount was manageable enough to be repaid from their existing income if necessary

Case Study #2: Business Start-Up (Construction Innovation)

A software engineer approached me with a relatively new concept for building residential homes. I wasn't initially optimistic—a software engineer attempting to revolutionize the home building industry seemed like a stretch.

However, he had done his homework and worked with a reputable accountant I knew to develop a solid business plan. I was impressed, though still not entirely convinced.

He needed over $1,250,000 to purchase a building and equipment, plus working capital to sustain operations until he could establish the business and market his concept.

It was ambitious, but his business plan appeared sound. He had identified his market, pricing strategy, demand level, and sales approach. All bases seemed covered. While the owner lacked direct building industry experience, his business plan addressed this by bringing in relevant experts when needed, particularly in sales.

The next hurdle was the down payment for the building and equipment. Banks typically want borrowers to contribute at least 25% of the purchase price, financing the remainder.

In this case, the borrower had only about 15% of the purchase price and approximately three months of operating capital—short of the six months banks usually prefer for the start-up phase.

The Solution

We paired a conventional bank loan with an SBA 504 loan. This allowed the borrower to proceed with just 15% down and three months of working capital during start-up.

The SBA 504 loan enters the picture after the bank has funded the initial purchase of the building and equipment. It then pays off 40% of the bank loan and takes a secondary lien position on the collateral.

This arrangement strengthened the bank's position in the collateral being used as security. Instead of having a loan of $1,062,500 against the building and equipment, the bank's exposure was reduced to $637,500—approximately 50% of the assets' value.

If the venture failed to meet projections and the bank had to foreclose, they would have much more cushion in the collateral value to recover the loan. If the building and equipment didn't sell for enough to pay off both the bank and the SBA, the SBA would absorb the shortfall.

The Outcome

The business didn't succeed as planned—in fact, it fizzled. However, the borrower recognized early that it wasn't working and proactively sold the building and equipment, generating enough to repay both the bank and the SBA.

Nothing is guaranteed, but he secured the loan based on his strong business plan (despite its ultimate failure) and the collateral pledged—along with the SBA 504 loan making up the difference.

He got the loan because we established clear repayment assurances from the beginning. Without these safeguards, the loan would never have been approved.

Case Study #3: Business Start-Up (Vending Machines)

A schoolteacher came to me seeking funding to purchase two vending machines as a way to supplement her income.

She was well-prepared with a good business plan and had sufficient funds for the required 25% down payment. But there was one significant problem.

Her business plan hadn't adequately considered the competition. Similar vending machines already occupied the prime locations throughout the city. Another provider had effectively captured the entire market.

The teacher wanted to enter this business precisely because the existing operation appeared successful.

The loan amount was modest—only $35,000—and through her teaching income, she could repay it without much difficulty even if the venture failed. The machines were generic enough that they could be resold to recover most, if not all, of the bank's investment if necessary.

The Outcome

Despite these positive factors, I declined the loan. The reason? Competition. You cannot expect to challenge an entrenched competitor using the same approach they use and expect to succeed.

I couldn't in good conscience approve a loan for a venture with a greater than 95% likelihood of failure, even though the borrower could repay regardless of the outcome.

Case Study #4: Business Expansion (Real Estate Development)

A builder I had previously financed for several home construction projects approached me about a loan to purchase land. He planned to develop a subdivision, then build and sell homes on all the lots.

It was a solid plan. He had proven experience in home building with a successful track record. There was just one problem: he wanted to jump from $400,000 loans for individual projects to a loan exceeding $2,500,000.

The builder had the necessary skills but lacked the financial strength to weather market fluctuations. If home sales slowed even slightly, he wouldn't be able to meet interest payments on the larger loan. He was financially capable of handling interest on the smaller loans but not on the larger commitment.

The Solution

Based on my experience with this builder—knowing him to be capable, efficient, intelligent, and determined to succeed—I suggested he find a partner who could provide the financial strength he lacked. This partner would guarantee his loans in exchange for a share of the profits.

The builder followed this advice. He carefully selected a partner looking to invest with a young, energetic entrepreneur who could put his money to productive use in exchange for profit participation.

The partner not only guaranteed the loan but also provided additional capital to purchase more land, expanding the project's scope while reducing risk since cash rather than borrowed funds was used for the additional acquisition.

The Outcome

The partnership proved highly successful for both parties. They developed several subdivisions together, and the builder grew his operation to the point where other potential financial partners approached him with opportunities. He eventually gained the ability to select his partners.

Ultimately, he became successful enough to undertake projects independently (which I financed), while continuing to finance his home building operation.

He expanded from building 3-5 homes annually to over 100 homes per year without substantially increasing his risk. He also generated excellent returns for his financial partners along the way.

Why He Got the Initial Loan

- He had proven experience in his field
- He had a solid plan and thorough knowledge of the market and competition
- He was already competing successfully in the market
- He found a financial partner to compensate for his weakness—insufficient financial strength to carry loan payments during potential sales slowdowns

Case Study #5: Bridge Funding (Luxury Home Construction)

A home designer/builder approached me with a problem. He had designed and built a dream home but had become so engrossed in the design and construction that he went severely over budget and exhausted his personal funds before completing the project.

His plan was to finish construction and showcase the home in a community Parade of Homes event—excellent advertising for his design/build business. He was confident that afterward, he could sell the home for a substantial profit, repay any bank financing, and keep a sizeable return for himself.

The challenge was that he lacked sufficient existing income to make interest payments on any bank loan. The bank could potentially defer interest payments until the home sold, but this represented significant risk.

What if the home didn't sell for the asking price? The bank would lose its loan funds, and the borrower lacked the financial strength to cover any shortfall. He had invested everything in this single project. If it failed, his business would collapse, and the bank would take a loss.

The builder had a reasonable track record, though not perfect. He had struggled with similar projects previously, and other banks had faced repayment challenges. As a banker, I declined to make the loan—the risk was simply too high.

The Solution

However, I knew investors willing to take chances on such projects with the prospect of higher returns. The higher the risk, the higher the potential return needed for any investment.

I connected the designer/builder with these investors. They offered him a one-year loan with sufficient funding to complete the home, but at an interest rate 3% higher than bank financing. Despite the premium, it was worthwhile for the builder.

The Outcome

He completed the home, featured it in the Parade of Homes and... it didn't sell.

This could have been disastrous. However, the designer/builder had invested enough of his own money that the investors weren't overly concerned. The home appraised at $3,100,000, while the loan amount was $1,250,000. With the interest rate at 12%, the investors were satisfied with their return. There was no need to panic yet.

After several months without a sale, the designer/builder moved into the home—it was, after all, his dream home. The investors remained unconcerned, as there was still substantial equity between the home's value and their loan amount. In fact, they were content with the extended timeframe because they were earning an excellent return on what they considered adequately secured capital.

Six months later, the designer/builder secured long-term financing to remain in the home permanently. He paid off the investors, and everyone was satisfied. For the builder, the higher interest cost was worth it to complete and ultimately keep his dream home.

This exemplifies alternative financing options. If a bank declines your application due to weaknesses, consider private sources or partners to address those shortcomings. Don't overlook these possibilities.

Case Study #6: Large Real Estate Development (Shopping Center)

I've included this example for two reasons: it's an interesting story, and it teaches valuable lessons about making projects work through persistence and determination.

A twenty-something real estate agent approached me with plans to finance a large retail shopping center from the ground up. His plan was excellent, but he had no money for a down payment and no experience with projects of this magnitude.

The proposed shopping center would include two restaurant pads, two large anchor tenants, and numerous smaller retail spaces—easily a $10,000,000 project. Until this point, the young agent had only sold residential properties. He was a dreamer, but his dream had potential.

He had secured an excellent property perfectly suited for this development by agreeing to pay a premium on the land price. This arrangement motivated the landowners to work with him. They would receive a premium price if the development succeeded; if the agent couldn't secure financing, his planning work would only enhance the land's value—a win-win for the sellers if they remained patient.

The agent had invested his own money to work with an engineer/designer to create the site plan. He had initiated discussions with the city for approvals, and the design was good enough that the city liked it and was moving toward approving the site plan. The zoning was already appropriate.

He had also approached several large retailers he believed would want to locate at the site, as well as restaurants interested in purchasing the designated restaurant pads.

Clearly, this young real estate agent was not just a dreamer but also a doer.

By the time he came to me, he had letters of intent for the purchase of a restaurant pad and commitments from the two anchor tenants.

My evaluation indicated the project could succeed if everything proceeded according to plan—which, in my experience, rarely happens.

The Challenges

Despite his progress, the real estate agent lacked several critical elements:

1. A down payment (or equity) of 25% of the project's cost/value
2. Sufficient cash reserves to handle unforeseen problems that inevitably arise
3. Adequate financial strength to sustain the project if leasing progressed slower than anticipated
4. Relevant experience in developing and managing a project of this size

The Solution

We recommended the young agent find a partner with the necessary financial strength, cash, and experience to join him on the project.

Never one to give up, and with our encouragement (because we liked what he had assembled), he found a financial partner with the required experience and financial strength. However, this partner still lacked the necessary cash to make it work.

This missing element was critical—insufficient cash for launching the project was a deal-breaker for the bank.

While discussing this with my boss—a seasoned business banker with nearly 30 years' experience (whereas at that time I had only been a commercial lender for about two years)—he devised a solution.

Rather than requiring the borrowers (the young agent and his financial partner) to have cash upfront, the bank would allow the cash to come from the sale of the restaurant pad. This would occur in a simultaneous closing that included the loan, the restaurant pad sale, and the initial funding of the development loan to pay the landowners.

The Outcome

The young real estate agent had assembled all the pieces, and everything closed simultaneously. The necessary cash was obtained, the land sellers received their premium price, the restaurant secured their desired pad, and the bank provided the development loan for the shopping center.

The young agent, still in his early twenties, became the owner of a highly successful retail development on prime real estate. From his initial investment of approximately $25,000 and a year of hard, diligent, and intelligent work, he secured an annual income of nearly $150,000. His partner also received $150,000 annually simply for providing advice and signing the loan.

This might seem like a lot for the young agent to sacrifice for his partner's minimal contribution. But half of something significant is far better than all of *nothing*. I know the young agent was delighted with the result. Wouldn't you be?

Why He Got the Loan

The young real estate agent had assembled all components necessary for the bank to stretch its normal parameters and approve the loan. He worked hard, found solutions (with help) for his deficiencies, and persisted until everything came together.

In short, creativity, tenacity, and hard work earned him a lifetime annual income that would increase over time as rents increased.

He didn't take an enormous risk, nor did the bank. The person assuming the greatest risk was actually the financial partner who staked his personal financial strength to guarantee the loan until the project was developed. Now you understand why he received half the proceeds.

Chapter 12: Conclusion

If you want to secure a business loan, you must demonstrate three critical elements:

1. **Show the bank unequivocally how they will be repaid**
2. **Demonstrate why YOU are the right person to complete the project**
3. **Provide sufficient collateral/security for the loan in case things don't go as planned**

Would you lend significant amounts of your own money to a stranger who doesn't meet these three criteria? I didn't think so.

That's exactly how bankers view loan applications. If you develop solid ways to satisfy these three criteria, you'll always get the financing you need.

Securing financing requires hard work but is well worth the effort. A strong business/financing plan will typically find the necessary funding. It will also help you evaluate your business's worth. The process of compiling this information helps identify weaknesses and strengths that you can address to enhance your business's value.

Now get going!

Get your business financed!

If you want personal help with your loan package, reach out to me at hbstucki1@gmail.com and write in the subject line, "Let's Talk Loans." I'll reply to set up a free consultation.

If you liked this book, please do me a favor, and leave a review. Your words help share my message with others who may also enjoy it. Your support is greatly appreciated. Click HERE to leave a review.

Be sure to check out other work by Brad Stucki at www.amazon.com/author/hbstucki. Free downloads are often available. Also, click "Follow" on the Author Page to be notified of new releases.

About the Author:
H. Bradley Stucki has been a director in three different investment companies, a Senior Vice President at a bank, and owns three businesses.

He helped pioneer the concept of "Business Incubation" and worked with over 250 fledgling companies helping them grow and flourish while still early in his career.

He was born and raised in southern Utah with horses, cows and other assorted pets. He is the third of six children and survived childhood only by utilizing an active imagination. His hobbies include reading and travel. His hobbies include reading and travel. He and his wife live in a high mountain valley, population 250 (more or less).

www.ingramcontent.com/pod-product-compliance
Lightning Source LLC
Chambersburg PA
CBHW021503210526
45463CB00002B/874